Short Stories

7 SOUTH AFRICAN POETS

Poems of exile
collected and selected
by Cosmo Pieterse

HEINEMANN
LONDON IBADAN NAIROBI LUSAKA

Heinemann Educational Books Ltd
48 Charles Street, London W1X 8AH
P.M.B. 5205 Ibadan · P.O.B. 45314 Nairobi
P.O. Box 3966 Lusaka
EDINBURGH MELBOURNE AUCKLAND KINGSTON TORONTO
HONG KONG SINGAPORE KUALA LUMPUR NEW DELHI

ISBN 0 435 90064 1

Distributed in the U.S.A.
by Humanities Press, Inc.
New York, N.Y.

Half-title illustration
by Dumile

Set in Monotype Bembo
Printed Offset Litho and bound in Great Britain by
Cox & Wyman Ltd, London, Fakenham and Reading

Contents

[v]

CONTENTS

CONTENTS

CONTENTS

Acknowledgements

My profound thanks are due to:
the poets for their contributions and patience; the publishers
for their patience and understanding, particularly to James
Currey for his constant encouragement, help and prodding;
Miss Pacey for her invaluable assistance in preparing the bulk
of the manuscript, and also to her willing pool of typists
whose practice made perfect pages, especially Harriet, Julia
and B.H.; and finally to all publications in whose pages the
poems of the present collection already have appeared.

Every care has been taken to trace copyrighted material to
the holders. Acknowledgement is made at the end of each
biography to journals and radio networks when poems by the
poet have been published or read.

Preface

This collection gives a taste of seven South African poets. Two of them, Dennis Brutus and Keorapetse Kgositsile, are committed and established as poets: Kgositsile has published a volume and has another due to appear; Brutus has published two volumes and has a third in preparation. The other five have had poems published in various anthologies and/or magazines.

To some extent, this collection covers the middle ground between the individual volume and the anthology. It presents seven contemporary poets from South Africa who write chiefly in English. These poets and their work focus attention on, and perhaps encourage the reader to reassess, two central facts of the South African English language writer's existence.

First, many South African writers, from Olive Schreiner to Don Jacobson, have had to leave South Africa to find their fame – and, some would say, their feet. South African writing in English stands significantly in the sign of exile. It is easy to choose a dozen names at random among South African poets who now live and often write outside their country of birth: William Plomer, Anthony Delius, Sydney Clouts, Mazisi Kunene, Breyten Breytenbach, Jeni Couzyn, Lewis Nkosi, Tulley Potter, Bloke Modisane, Ezekiel Mphahlele and Elizabeth Eybers. Their reasons for exile are various; they include South Africa's political climate, the Republic's censorship, the available audience, the need to pit oneself against international standards. Sometimes the exile is self-imposed; sometimes it is enforced: but it is exile, not the grand global tour. As a result, much South African poetry is now a poetry of the committed exile, the work of the 'ex'-South African who writes, not, as many earlier South African poets did, with a sense of spiritual exile from a European home, but out of a conviction that something is rotten under the Southern Cross.

And so, secondly, as can be seen from this collection, much South African poetry is charged with protest. It represents various points around the compass of the politically conscious writer. There are the political activists who have suffered trial, injury, torture and prison; there are those who have experienced artistic strangulation and personal humiliation; there are others who saw and felt. Some of these poems were written at home, some in exile. But in general, their point of departure is public concern and their value, social compassion.

This collection brings to mind many questions– does South African poetry become 'shrill, hysterical, thinly disguised political propaganda?' Is it bad for the poetic product if this element is an important ingredient? Does exile affect the poet's vision, style, range and diction? How do these South Africans compare with the poets of Angola and Mozambique? How does exile affect a poet? It is certainly not the intention of this volume to answer these questions. But it is hoped that the reader who is interested by such questions will be stimulated and helped by this collection.

Above all, this volume, while not claiming to represent the poets, does present them as individuals. Their work may have qualities in common, as some aspects of their lives have; but they do not form a 'school', nor does their work show any trend. These are, simply, seven poets from South Africa.

Cosmo Pieterse
London

Dollar Brand

Africa, Music and Show Business
An analytical survey
in twelve tones
plus finale

I

geography

> so many theories of east and west abound
> one thing is certain though
> this earth
> is round

II

slave bell

> slave
> master your bell
> your master
> like the cat
> was belled
> with time
> no clocks
> no clime
> stipulate
> late afternoon
> nor early mourning for the dead
> sombre tolls the very same bell that rings for joy
> bell
> slave
> time is your master

III

spiritual

> when i get to heaven gonna play on my harp
> gonna play all over god's heaven
>
> but only with the cats who can make the changes

IV

western influence

> my baybee eesah cryink baa baa
>   forra me
> i geef her de mango
> i geef her de banana
> but she's stillah cryink baa baa
>   forra me

V

rhythm afrique

> joey had the biggest feet
> so he played tenor

VI

blues for district six

early one new year's morning
when the emerald bay waved its clear waters against the noisy
   dockyard
a restless south easter skipped over slumbering lion's head
danced up hanover street
tenored a bawdy banjo
strung an ancient cello
bridged a host of guitars
tambourined through a dingy alley
into a scented cobwebbed room
and crackled the sixth sensed district
into a blazing swamp fire of satin sound

early one new year's morning
when the moaning bay mourned its murky waters against the
   deserted dockyard
a bloodthirsty south easter roared over hungry lion's head
and ghosted its way up hanover street
empty
forlorn
and cobwebbed with gloom

VII

where loneliness' still waters meet nostalgia
and morning breaks the city sun and smoke
and towering grey the buildings murmur
grim subway rumblings in their roots
i scan the vacant faces and sad smiles
and long for home

the night my soul had herringed red
through raucous songs of childhood:
and friends and comic stories long forgotten
were whiskied out of memories dim
to function as narcotic
and silence cruel reality as it screamed
it's neither here nor there

i'm hemisphered
but three
the southern cross and libran scale
and god knows
he knows
where

VIII

ballet for tired sons and lovers

figure belt – is the tragedy of the illustrious son of a suburban
african chief who, disillusioned by the apparent ineffectiveness
of his magical beadwork, discards his girds and elopes with a
fast-travelling-northbound-salesgirl.
After mesmerizing him with her hypnotic, synthetic orna-
ments, she locks him up in a fashion magazine and in order to
keep him amused, content and in her power, she clads him
with so many figure belts that he stifles and loses his voice and
in final desperation strangles himself and dies.

IX

wind up

the southern spring winds
myself in two
one wintered in cold steel northern city
brittle eyed neon guards my empty stomach
the other
a dimming summer
camera-ed in youth
and matinéed each minute of each dreary day

X

double cross

> in the morning came white dressed white men in a big white
>   car
> they took him away
>
> in the afternoon came black dressed black men in a big black
>   car
> they took him away

XI

> the terrored dusk screams
> the land
> in the beginning
> love was
> the fuse igniting all
> clay
> and green leafed sun dynamoed my buck
> which now gallops petrified in the rumbling twilight
> through fields of empty stomachs' wide eyed plea
> to where the midnight hides
> dark robed three armed inevitable
> one hand outstretched towards a pair of fleeing balances
> one empty hour glassed
> and last
> a bloodied feather falling from a palsied palm

XII

the harmonica

it has been raining
and in the gutter lies the harmonica
gurgling incoherently

the man stooped
to retrieve the instrument
and it obeyed and played

the people heard and loved him

he dwelt in skyscrapers and blew wind
and soon his feet became unsteady

one morning when he came down to dig his senses
it was too late
the pavement loomed up and cracked him violently in the head
and the children ran away with bits of his brain

and the harmonica rattled back into the gutter where it had
    fallen
with the inauguration of time

FINALE

life in a national park/or – take five

    last night two monkeys stumbled onto an
    AMAZING
    COLOSSAL
    FANTASTIC
    secret

    on the outskirts of an african village
    where they had been sleeping off a drunken stupor
    they discovered an ancient clock
    ticking away in $1979\frac{1}{4}/35\frac{1}{2}$
    (they worked it out)

    they were jubilant

    after much deliberation
    as to who the rightful owner was
    (they even casted lots)
    they finally decided that the whole world should know of this
    amazing phenomenon and that by using their usual 'pay-while-
    you-hear' ritual, they could ensure themselves a life time of
    happiness and if it came to the push they would
    DISCOVER
    EXCAVATE
    and even
    INVENT
    more clocks

    this morning for some obscure reason (they thought)
    the clock decided to change to 4/4

    [10]

they were furious

learned gorillas were called in on this appalling example of
   disobedience

the suggestion that the clock's mechanism be studied was
   accepted, half heartedly

but alas, it was too late
for when they touched the spring, there occurred a terrifying
   explosion
and the whole monkey kingdom was blown to bits

the resultant itch woke up TIME
and she scratched vaguely under her armpit

Dennis Brutus

Climates of Love
and Continents

Lutuli : December 10th 1961

The African lion rouses from his shadowy lair
   and roars his challenge through the clamorous earth:
   – its billow blots all discords and all jars.

Hippo and elephant and buffalo without dispute
   go lumbering to the drinking pools:
   – but all the land he views he rules:

From here he pads on sun-picked bone and brittle thorn
   sniffing the tawny skies of a new day:
   – power ripples over him like the light of dawn.

Miles of my arid earth
rasping dry as smoker's cough and craving
heat, hunger ache in your dusty haze
sighing, heaving, tremulous;

all my seared eyes caress your miles –
boulders that blister, scald and rust –
ranging parched reaches of rutted sands;
coax pastels from your dun and dust

and know the tenderness
of these my reaching hands
can conjure moisture, gentleness
and honey sweetness from your yearning hollows.

Greenness
balms the eyes
the senses and the mind,
the hurt
of pounded feet:

in her infinite variety
of shades
of subtly-cadenced greens
lies part
of England's dearness

✤

By the waters of Babylon
>   the brackish wastes of alienness
>   lie like dust on heart and throat,
>   contour and curve of hill and field
>   unspeaking and meaningless
>   as a barbarous foreign tongue

by the waters of Babylon
we sat down and wept
>   the mind yearns over the low horizon
>   to other familiar friendly haunts
>   not unlike these gracious scenes

when we remembered thee
O Zion
>   these trees; these hills; this sky, this sun
>   evoke a dearness that lacerates;
>   the heart heels from this wounding loveliness

how can we sing our songs
in a strange land?
>   wordlessly
>   one turns from such beauty and such pain:
>   weeps.

In a strange land.
By the waters of Babylon
we sat down
and wept.

(Bamako, Mali.)

[18]

Milkblue-tender the moonlit midnight sky;
receive me now my sleeping love.
Lovelaughter-gentle, a luminous glow
arches from circling horizoning hills
to this plain your tremulous breast exposes:

So, gentle and tender I brood and bow
over your scent, your hid springs of mirth
and know
here in this dusk, secret and still
I can bend and kiss you now, my earth.

I am the tree
creaking in the wind
outside in the night
twisted and stubborn:

I am the sheet
of the twisted tin shack
grating in the wind
in a shrill sad protest:

I am the voice
crying the night
that cries endlessly
and will not be consoled.

The yellow gorse is out
and flames along the hillsides –
puddles and splashes along the hills
and smouldering brushfires of gold

I walk in the English quicksilver dusk
and spread my hands to the soft spring rain
and see the streetlights gild the flowering trees
and the late light breaking through patches of broken cloud
and I think of the Island's desolate dusks
and the swish of the Island's haunting rain
and the desperate frenzy straining our prisoned breasts:
and the men who are still there crouching now
in the grey cells, on the grey floors, stubborn and bowed.

In the dove-grey dove-soft dusk
when the walls softened to frozen smoke
and their rigidity melted
receding to miles,
when the air was alive and tender
with a mist of spray from the sea,
the air luminous
and the sky bright with the dulling glimmer
of cooling molten lead;
when the island breathed –
trees, grass, stones and sand breathing
quietly at the end of the long hot day –
and the sea was a soft circling presence –
no longer a tight barbed menacing ring:
in the dusk
nothing was more agonizing than to be seized
by the poignant urgent simple desire
simply to stroll in the quiet dusk:
as I do now:
as I do now, and they do not.

En Route

Sixty packed in a truck
we sat or crouched or perched or squatted
warm shoulders, hips, elbows, knees
squeezed and jostled in the pre-dawn dark
forced into contorted postures by the chains
talking, laughing, reminiscing, telling tales
cheering each other with courageous exhortations
or stilled as the heart was clutched by grim forebodings:
and suddenly the sky-rim blazing with flame and blood
while from the dusk flowered the friendly faces.

They backed the truck
right up to the huge door in the massive walls
while a crowd –
gathered for some other reason—
jostled round:

then through the fort:
crenellated, intricate and inter-locking
as the traditional fortress
– historic monument, no doubt,
to wars I remember with disgust.

Then in the parade-ground enclosure
to squat, chained on the gravel
in the slowly basking sun
and wait for mealies
or hobble to the can in the corner
while a drunk African warder
tried to provoke an argument

(In a reflecting window
I discovered the horror of my own appearance)

The old building
with the mannerisms of a bygone air
exuded age, reeked history

And we too were history.

Over the thunder-heads of terror we may fly
as now I probe their structure from head to base
from the Thor-hammerhead of their crown
thrashing through their configuration
like a sexually masterful invasion:

and if there is power and grace for this,
then I dare believe there will be ways
to find so great a height and peace
without the thunderclaps and storms
that will burst my land with cataclysmic blood.

At noon we were heeling northward
and our shadow pointed to the sun

grey-green on the rimpled water
flung aslant by the sun

far far below
like a shadowy arrow or whale:

the twice-blue Caribbean
mocked, foam-flecked, the Mediterranean:

then without effort we were lordly
and the first cloud-wisps swam by.

Christmas 1965

Through the bruises and the spittle.
the miasma of invective
and the scaled refractions of our prejudice
painfully man emerges.

Straw, shavings, hay
and the mist of the cows' cloudbreath:
and through it flickered the lambence
of man's inherent divinity.

Being the mother of God
you need not overly concern
yourself with such a churlish child
– indeed might well dispense
with such a bad-mannered son:

So I must beg you to excuse
any inattention and neglect of you
in the midst of what is really your event
and hope that you will accept my anxious thought
and planning for the joy of others
as something which is really yours.

I. Choonara

Scenes from a Cell

Response

Then
  As now
    When
   Fingerstouched
       You
     Moved
   Your
  Hand

      Away.

Oh, to be free, white, and twenty-one;
Now that the jacarandas are in bloom.

A Monday Morning in March

Morning crawls out in striped pyjamas
Feels the cold floor
And draws the curtains
To blue skies, chirping birds
And downy frost
Clinging to glints of glistening green.

Cheerful goodmorning of the milkman
Rattles along with his bottles from door to door,
Races against the young lad
Hurrying with the morning papers.

Pale and tired the moon looks
From last night's dreams, and joins
The daffodils mocking the morning sun.
Crocuses lie limp from weekend glory,
Almond blossoms blush pink
And frying breakfast-smell
Waits in the doorway for the postman.

London wakes up
To the slow grind of cars, buses
And clickety-clack clickety-clack
Of suburban trains.

Cups of coffee grow cold
Rivalling for attention with press studs
And lipstick cases.
Monday's hairdo is not as pretty as Saturday's:
Quick brush and six hair pins
Bend it into a polite inoffensive style.

Then off to work
In folded queues
Inch by inch past the booking clerk,
And in folded queues, necks craned
Past the glaring morning papers
Towards the empty number two to Victoria.

Cats crawl out, bask on window sills,
Dogs sniff gateposts, trees, other dogs,
And petrol attendants feed hungry cars.

Girls run for buses.
Shopkeepers dust their wares.
Fruitsellers arrange orange pyramids.
Butchers cut meat.
Mothers push prams.
Fathers peck goodbyes.
Children go to school.

In cells prisoners envy
Prisoners outside.

On Streatham Common

Dusk falls, creeps on plimsolls.
Distance is lights, pinpoints
Like grounded stars
And cars as moving ants
Hurrying, scurrying in anonymous streams.
Pond is a mirror
To inverted trees,
Garden gate's locked.
Horizon is lights.
Jupiter glides, hides behind misty view.
Dusk is gray
And cars little blobs of red,
And buses moving flats,
Train's a snake with light.
Smoke and chimney and sky are one
As evening folds into night.

Soliloquy

Do not begrudge
This one-grain happiness,
This red-robin reality.
What is yours?
Gin and tonic,
Beer shampoo froths,
Silk shantung shirt hides
The appendix scar.
Tin medal rattles,
Rat-tat-tat-tat. Another
plane is down.
Mascara runs in rain
or tears.
Gin and tonic, sir.
Twisted tongue twister.
Double gin, did you say,
Lingfield's off, frozen.
Bingo on Tuesdays only.
Nothing on telly?
Hi-fi has packed up.
Another gin.
Lingfield's off, frozen.
Smoke?
No, I do not
Smoke
Ciga-
rettes
any
more.
Single-grained soliloquy.
Illusion? Reality?
What is yours.
Gin and tonic.

Lingfield's off.
Pâté de foie gras?
Needle.
Nothing
more.
Just one jab,
And again, and again, and again.

Asylum

They stand there
Shrouded in starch-white
Silent smiles glued
To the faces:
That straightjacketted response
To the world.
And I look on
Smiling
My sad smile.
Inward is the only asylum
After the womb.

I am going to make
An upside down cake.
I know I'll need some flour,
But I am going to wait
At least half an hour
Before I begin to bake.

I'll need some fat
And eggs, and water,
Sugar in an upside down bowl
And mix all of that.

Before I can really begin
I'll need an upside down tin,
And an upside down oven
To fit everything in.

I know, you will say
I will have to stand on my head
To eat an upside down cake.
But I have thought of that:
I will choke and be dead.

So I will change my mind
And bake instead
A sideways cake
And eat it
Sideways in bed.

Letter to Mamma

Do not ask me
why we are here, mamma.
That is an irrelevancy.
We cannot tell
the difference
between the North,
the South.
Neither could grand-pa back home
A hundred years ago
when he was a child.
If it moves
we shoot
straight between the
slanty eyes.
That it is the enemy
of the ideal we are defending.
Do not ask me why.

Fred. You know Fred, mom.
Remember Fred. He is dead.
And Bill was killed on the hill.
Some others you know mom
are gone.
But we go on, and on, and on.
We are defending an ideal.
We know it does not sound real,
but here we see clear
the yellow peril in the green jungle
and the red peril in the green jungle,
the flies besides, and the mosquitoes,
the swamps, and the riverboats.
Then there are the bombs, booby traps, bazookas
and a sniper's bullet to stop you dead

in your tracks, mom. Remember Fred.
But we still stick fast, mamma
because we are defending
the Great Ideal.
But it is so far away from home, mamma,
so far from ideal.

Gaza '67

The dead lie dead on desert sand
A curly strand of hair
Clots.
A gleeful glow
In some gunsmith show:
They will be back
After prayers,
After washing the dead
For another round, another round.

Quick
The death salesmen are at the door
Mamma, please buy me a gun.

❖

I am the king
You will come
Wearing
Just a whisper
Of perfume.

The winds roll down the mountain
The winds make and break the mountains
The trees shiver and shake
The leaves quiver and shake
As the winds roll down the mountains.

Dressed in a glimmer of gold you come to me
Dressed in a glimmer of gold you come to me
Dressed in a glimmer of modesty you come to me
Dressed in a glimmer of smile you come to me.

The rivers roll down the valleys
The rivers wind, grind down the valleys
Rushing
    Gushing
        Turning
           Twisting
       Winding
            Finding their way
                To the sea.

Dressed in the finest silks and satins
Dressed in the finest silks and satins
You walk quietly
In the finest silk and satin
There beside me.

[45]

Clouds gather and grumble
Gather and rumble, stumble
Shout and shriek
Burst asunder
Weep
Tears
Fears
Lightning shriek, clap and thunder

In silent love
There beside me
In silent love
You come
There beside me

Forests on fire, flames and ashes
Forests on fire, flames and ashes
Night day melt merge urge into one
Flames crackle, spit
Dance, shriek, shout
Leaves char, grumble
Twigs twist, tumble
Branches crack, crumble
Stumps stumble.

I the king
You
Wearing
Just a whisper of perfume.

Naked, modest, silent shame
A whisper your name
Blush breaks asunder

Eyes fall, find the floor
The door is silent evermore
The door that let you in
A moment ago
Is shut a moment evermore and evermore.

The wind whispers behind the curtains
The wind peeps from behind the curtains
Walls watch in silence
Light leaves by the window
Darkness and I are one
You and I are one
All that is one is one.

Birds sing, flowers sway
Forests grow, rivers run
Sea spray
Tides come, call
Ebb, fall
Sea shouts, shrieks, roars, rises, runs
Back
And back again.
Cliffs edge slowly to sea
Pebbles dash, rattle, roll
Footsteps echo the crunch crunch
Sound, noise, music all scream
For that lost moment
A moment ago.

I am the king:
Solitary, stately,
Deemed wise,
Otherwise insignificant

Save for the shifting
Of a single pebble.
The tide covers everything
Including
The nakedness beside me
Inside me.

Silk and satin lie crumpled on the floor
Silk and satin lie crumpled near the door
Wind whistles beyond the window
Wind whistles beyond the door.

Your breasts are the mountains
Your body the sea
Raging, raving, fighting,
Locked in a sea of storm.
Your body is a forest on fire
Heaving, hugging, crackling
Angry mountain on fire.

The wind whispers from behind the curtains.

Trees topple, cliffs topple
Columns topple, crowns topple
This island on fire.

The wind peeps from behind the curtains.

Lips weary with weariness
Lips wet and weary with weariness
Eyes wet and weary with weariness
Tears, fears of desire
Shaking, shivering desire
Exhausting exhaustion of desire.

[48]

I. CHOONARA

The wind whistles from behind the curtains.

Silks and satins, crumpled on the floor
Doors locked evermore, evermore.
Forests grow inside you
Mountains grow inside you
Seed grows inside you
Waters rush, roar, break
Inside you.

Pale is the moon that shines from behind the curtains.

Hand stretches, fetches
Silks and satins
Grips the silks and satins
Fingers the cold silks and satins
Leave, let go the silks and satins.
Nakedness is there inside you
Inside you.

Forests fume
Seas storm
Mountains roar
Silence
Is inside you
Inside you.

I am the king
Naked and silent
There beside you
Naked and silent
Inside you
Inside you.

C. J. Driver

*Elegies
of Light*

Elegy for my Contemporaries

Bones on a telegraph-pole
Dance their epitaph
To those born rich and healthy,

Young men, clean-limbed, clear-eyed,
Those who wore the clothes
Of dying children.

They were not without love
Or beauty; their hands were tied
To the wheels of brilliance

And they whirled like gunfire
In the night. I name them
Among my friends, my people,

Those who married well, who loved
Their children, who gave
What their pockets allowed.

They shall die in their doorways
And in the streets, thrombosis
And murder pay their debts –

You cannot count them now, the lines
Of soldiers who drank deeply
From the jewelled cup of safety.

Afternoon in an African Township

Langa: in memory of Ernest Galo

Iron makes my roof,
Stones my fences.
Doors stand free
Of cluttering.

Do not say more
Than the simple
I am hungry
Or *This is stone.*

The streets do not run
With blood.
The houses
Are not burning.
There are on children.

A Ballad of Hunters

My great-grandfather hunted elephants,
Shot four hundred in a year,
Till one day his death turned round
And sniggered in his ear.

The theme's the same, the method changes –
Time has planned the ending,
Has turned the hunter to the hunted
And bred the next from nothing.

My great-great-uncle farmed alone,
Made next to nothing from his land,
Till at last the cancer took him,
Eating from his living hand.

The theme's the same, the method changes –
Time has planned the ending,
Has turned the farmer to the harvest
And bred the next from nothing.

Cousins and cousins in their dozens
Were killed in their mission churches
By the tribes whose heads they broke
To teach them the Christian virtues.

The theme's the same, the method changes –
Time has planned the ending,
Has turned the clergy to the converts
And bred the next from nothing.

My father's father died at Delville Wood,
Shooting Germans for his British past –
Left his wife a private's pension
And children to make it last.

The theme's the same, the method changes –
Time has planned the ending,
Has turned the sniper to the target
And bred the next from nothing.

Both my uncles fought the war,
Like lovers died a year apart –
Left some letters and a flag or two
And silence to be their art.

The theme's the same, the method changes –
Time has planned the ending,
Has turned the fighters to the dying
And bred the next from nothing.

Now I'm my subject, a sort of hunter
Stalking the blood of my family –
But hunted too by time's revenge
For all they made of my history.

The theme's the same, the method changes –
Time will plan the ending,
Will turn the hunter to the hunted
And breed the last from nothing.

A Love Song

Brittle as glass, my woman;
If I touch her she will break.
So do not come too close –
This is a most private place.

Under her left breast, on her palm,
I found my private marks –
She has made hers in my face,
Privately in that public place.

The hurt forms part of her beauty,
The scars breathe beauty themselves;
Nowadays I own nothing of her
But a brittle time of her flesh.

But will she ever let me free?
I am held by the glass of self
To her secret gaze of hurt
And her lovely privacy of flesh.

O do not come so close –
This is a most private place;
It's the traitor glass I cry for
That sees her in my face.

A Public Man Confesses his Private Longings

Bald mother moon and your children,
Bless my country, bless my continent,
Bless the white cattle in the lands
Where the tribes gather
And the green sea-branches
That wave over us.

Bless her silence, bless her loveliness,
Bless the hair that curls like a hand
Over her nakedness.

Bless my image
Of the witching girl, a stone's throw from the church,
Dying so quietly that no-one could hear
And the hero running, though her answer told him
That all the waters were closed round her head.

Shine like gold on the great snake's back
That bred us and bears our children
In the tall mountains we call home,
In whose quiet I shall be found,
Visionary, with the light around me,
And each existence moving light,
And each light stillness.

Guilt is inelegant. How purely the light burns
At my bedside; someone outside would say,
'That room's burning.' It is only the way
Light beats at the curtains; my way of looking
Is slower – the light reads the words of a book
On my knees. I read the light. The light burns.

One Way of Looking

for Ann

There's one way of looking that sees
An intricate wove of emotion
In every move of the leaves –
You can hardly tell them apart,
The death of desire, the urge of the seed.

I have moved out of sunlight – the woods
Are my intricate home, though my eyes
Were made for a distance, not my hands
For this detail of delicate bones.

There are places to lie in the warmth
Of these woods; but the dark always dark
Makes room for my blindness – you learn this
By touching, then sleep through the day.

Sometimes she wakes and she calls me.
I go by the sound, though my hands
Are always before me. She's gone by that time.
I am learning the different names of the trees
And, when I learn light, I shall see her.

The People of Darkness

For Harry Cohen

All this is guesswork, an order based on small fact
And word-lust. It will not break one bone of exile.

It is an easy way to disguise the flesh of despair
As a hesitation in the voice, a small diffidence,
When it would cry out, 'God save us, save us' –
For my gods are only words dressed up like poems.

Various marks stumble darkly on a white page.
They go, my brave explorers, across their continents
Into the green, green summer.
                                    There they shall rest.

Proudly my gods blow and puff their poor feathers.

Of Unknown Origin

Believe me, there are times
when I waking
look from my bed to the window
over a jungle of floor
too thick to be walked through.

My head in the waves, my head
in a tangle
of islands. Africa sings to me,
You are lost in the islands,
You drown in your yellowing bed.

Green are the spattering vines
on the shaking
fever trees; the malarial hedgerows
are eating the ditches. The law
is never to grow. I do.

Containment by self, says my bed;
if the jungle
comes creeping, you will be free.
The jungle comes creeping. My hands
are tied to my bed.

Poem for a higher degree

These days my home is
  out of the mountains,
an island, a street, a house
          on the edge
  of water green or brown
    as studies take us –

confused by light, by cold,
  by easy winds, those
by flood un-iced. The weir roars;
          the lock-gates
  are never undone. The ice states:
    easy it does.

All day the tanker loads
  its roar of oil
into next door's storage.
          All night I leave
  my curtains open, catch
    the water-light

against white walls and ceiling,
  blue sheets and blankets,
my safety house. All day I am drawn
          to the weir;
  all night I sleep
    in the tanker's void.

To the Dark, Singing

in memory of John Harris, who was executed in 1965, for sabotage and murder, and who went to his execution singing, 'We Shall Overcome'.

This man's no hero; mad, perhaps,
Killed an old woman and burned
A child's face to a white skull
So he might make a god out of pain
To free his country from the praise
Of a golden beast. But we are fools
Who dose our disease with hate,

    Though we sing when we die.

No praise then; and no prayer either –
For we are past the praying stage.
All prayers shout out too loudly
When one man goes alone to die
In a short falling, a short way
Through his little dark to the dark,

    Though he sings when he dies.

Each of us makes a separate peace
With the dark; he made his cruelly
Both ways, that his beast of fire
Might gobble the other golden beast
And that the sweet smell of flesh
Burning, burning, might crowd the gate
Where his country waits, unspeaking,

    Though it sang when he died.

[64]

I can see no beauty in this
Except that a man should sing
To his dark
Till the rope breaks his voice –

The flames burn white in his skull
And no one death repeats another,

    Though he sang when he died.

Poem on a bad night

for Maeder Osler

The wind behind my curtain pulses.
What if rain should break the glass
And scuttle down, drop by drop,
Into my eyes?
              My soul's a traveller
From the far white mountains
Come down, come down.

The night's all my own. I possess it
Cloud by cloud; the rain is falling,
The moon's already down. This is simple,
The roads of dark.
              I ask – *by whom am I*
Made to walk this dust? But no-one
Takes the light away.

The wind confuses rain and blood.
I have hoped too long for light
And light's simplicities. I hear them now
In every bone,
              the curve of light,
The curve of light again. By these
I made the rain my own.

The boat of my soul staggers.
The rain's all I own; cloud by cloud
It makes the sky. On the roads
The grey dust flares.
              Come the rain,
Come the rain again,
Blind the light away.

For the dead

in memory of my father who died in January 1964.

The dead lie in the hills,
A long way to walk to –

Where the dark of the trees
Takes the reach of the sky.

The dead lie in still water –
The wind does not touch them.

Their age is the silence of rock,
The water crumbling down.

Timothy Holmes

Translations from Africa

Conceit

With a memory for sights and sounds
Which men and even elephants lack
The tiny eyelet bird which perches
Singing on the traveller's back
Casts his glance to left and right
To take the shifting landscape in
Absorbing, noting, knowing too well
Each detail missed a mortal sin:

His task is set by the Eagle, Vee'd
Sky dolphin: and should he dare
To close his eyelid, rest the eye
He would be the eagle's fare.

At journey's end, and one by one,
He sings his observations out
In music so sweet, so shrill and clear
It puts to shame the Eagle's shout.

Unease

Brightly plumaged birds
Which do not sing
And green and golden grass
Too sharp to lie upon
Companion here our river:

Further down the stream
Where grass gives way
To bare but singing trees
And those bright birds
To warblers and their kin
No equal beauty for the eye
Is found:
    Yet upstream far
Storms rage all the day
Killing the nerve of ear and eye:

Where then, in this self-loving valley
Should the hedonistic eagle dwell?

Fear

The cold spot on the heart repeats
The klink-klink of a blacksmith plover's cry,
    Over lake waters
    Goodbye, goodbye.

Purple heron's doubled neck and wings
Unfold, fold, change, become the sedge;
    Cold wavelets lap
    The false shore's edge.

Stone chat, fish eagle, jacana, coucal, hawk,
Egret, pied crow, names that catch the eye;
    Words with more meaning
    Less confidently fly.

The cold spot on the heart repeats
Malignant fears of tadpole, beetle, bream:
    Within eye-beauty
    Predator's quenchless gleam.

The Fossil

The discoverer of a forty-eight foot
Crocodile beneath Sahara sands
Of the République du Niger
Unearthed a valuable fossil:

But what makes news, for me,
Was the fact that its shape,
From snarl to lash,
Was the same as its descendants!

The only difference, really,
Was its size, twice today's largest!
A re-incarnated conqueror,
Napoleon or Ghengis,
Would in our livingrooms
Probably pass for commonplace.

Lifegiver

Usually the lifegiver.
Usually prayed for
Twelve months of the year.

Dug from many-fathomed
Wells. Led to where
Diamonds have less value.

Blocked in dams. Forced
Through tunnels for power.
Watched, loved, admired.

Fine beauty, creator of beauty;
In one place a dead grey
Forest, standing in billowing
Fields of breathtaking green
Drowned unto ghostliness.

The Other Face

In a pinpoint of silence
(Hence the unbroken fluttering, jumping,
Buzzing, munching)
The great forest begins
To whisper its own history
Which birds, invertebrates
And mammals
Knowingly wish untold.

Rivers fear ice, which pins
Them, so their faces stop their winking,
Smiling, mouthing
And can be read, slowly,
Distrust increasing fear
With curses found for lyrics
In the craggy cuneiform
Of their alphabets.

A Ten-Liner

The undercut bank lunges
Across the current. Sure
As diamonds, millions
Of water molecules
Gnaw into soil and stone.

Who stands there, aware
For first, then second times
Of a shiver, a plop
As stonelets fall,
Admiring?

The Conquerors

The sweet song of robins,
Solos above an orchestra of green
(Thick lawn, deep leaves, rich water)
Catch the mind for instants
In the turning stream of evening
After the year's first rain.

But does perhaps this sound-and-feeling world
Where thoughts are captured, so,
Rest eggshell-thin around
An unborn babe with shape and being
To deaden robins' song, set leaves aquiver,
Cast a mist through jewelled water?

Conquest

One throw cutting the evening air,
A broken scream, a silent fall,
A bounce from scrub to rock and bush,
Finished a generation, left clear
For newcomer with plough and gun
The dew-bejewelled country, rich
In soil, trees, birds, red meat,
Rivers, the bounty of a kingly sun.

Three days before, the last tired clan
Of a lost people, four generations,
Were hunted from their eyrie; and ran
Up mountain slopes that quailed the kite –
Were followed by shouts and voices born
Six thousand miles away.

         Shot after shot
Felled ancestor, father, uncle, husband. Fright
Sent mother-wife to scale the highest bluff.

There two final deaths gave the country over
To strangers.

The Conquered

Refuged in secret places far from concourses,
Hidden near living rock, home among windiness,
A long breath self-promised into the future,
Peril came to our valley, shirring flat waters
With smoke, dust of ironstone, startling soft palates.

Viewing land fastnesses, western protectors,
Seeing on bronzed hill-curves filtered sunlight,
Our evening blaze a comfort, air-sweetener,
With a rush of starlings night was present:
On those distant clifftops, a line of fires lighted
Their smoke, a burnt bitter, towards us blown.

From both sides advancing portents of danger,
Choking encroachment, forewarnings confirmed,
Broad lanes to a future closed up with poisons.
Walls of our refuge draw us against them.
Pressed us right through them, hid us behind,
Leaving small shadows of us and our chattels
Painted upon them. For others.

Reaction to Conquest

Three blows from a steel axe
Broke through the heart
Of a rare, extinction-threatened tree
Which though standing yet
Browns to fall.

Such was the time of year
That tight-skinned berries,
Waiting to explode, dried too soon,
And clatter-clattered
To the ground.

Around the root-tops, naked once
Hungry grass has crept
Now moss, bark-feeding insects,
Woodpeckers, fungus,
Dark leaf-mould.

Ausonius

I

Your immediate worry is over;
The rough hike through the valley
And foot-by-foot clamber
Up a vertiginous escarpment
Have produced an undulating plain,
Replete with small lake, gentle
Trees, an ice-clear stream, rushes,
Melodious birds; a place to rest.

Dip your hot feet in water; cast
An eye back to all the gentlefolk
Who, battles over, empires lost or won,
Have settled to write their days
Away by riversides. But don't ask the question
We could now put their ghosts:
A dove on buzzard's eggs, absorbed,
Sits comfortably upon its breezy nest.

II

A fascination with rivers
And water: for high places
Or woodland closeness,
A loving of the earth's bemusing
Countenance: microscopic study
Of the here.
Around the water edges,
On the brink of heights,
At all the borders of a chosen
Small world, shimmers the symptom
Of a question, its details
Avoided from fear.

III

When the storm passed away
The weather prophets were puzzled
By its mildness: Compared
To hurricanes in other parts, at other
Times, it made no more than ripples
On the lake: in one or two
Places though, side eddies had
Caused damage not yet repaired.

In the days that followed
Benefits flowed in its wake:
The rivers had a scour-out,
Fishing improved: crops of corn, cotton,
Sugar, nuts, fruit, shot up; sunshine
On good soil means plenty: cattle
Flourished. For the better, was any difference
In the season. No thing despaired;

Not even the underling of farm
And factory; nor the gnawers, borers,
Chewers of growth, who in the springing
Upshoot had ample staple for lean bellies:
Cutworm, weevil and wilddog
Did well: there was room for all.
Doubters of weather-clemency asked
Unanswerably what the next season would bear.

IV

The lake is held, sixty miles away
By battlements of concrete: here
From a cottage at the shore, you see
A new golden beach, nudged

[83]

By bows of fishing boats, shaded
With tall savannah trees accommodating
In growth a sudden water-surfeit.
Offshore, islands crowned with trees
Waterbird crowned.
At evening, along the sightline
A ripple of breeze from the south
Welcomes you to needed drink,
And you love the sundown from the ease
Of canvas chairs; shade brings life:
A heron moves, crickets start, frogs,
The first bat, doves swooping in, egrets
On the move to bed. Ice crackles in your glass.

V

When the water broke away, millions
Of carrion birds came on the wind
To stuff their crops with fish before
Maggots and bacteria had them.

Wheeling round in ever-banking
Arcs, birds made the pall of smoke
More usual over burning forests.

The sun shone on, contributing
His appetite to cleaning up the mess.

Then farmers came back, with hoes.

Keorapetse Kgositsile

Elusive Poet
for People Moving

For Melba

Morning smiles
In your eye
Like a coy moment
Captured by an eternal
Noon and from yesterdays
I emerge naked
Like a Kimberley diamond
Full like Limpopo after rain
Singing your unumbered charms.

Manifesto

After the inevitable rebirth
There is only loneliness a necessary pain
As quiet as a deep lake
Whose waters from the eternal spring
Trace a straight path
Through the maze of centuries of colonial dreams
Awakening
Overturning
     (Were you there when
     They killed your heroes
     Where were you when
     They killed Lumumba
     Were you there when
     They killed Brother Malcolm)

Shotgun

Five deaths ago my
Name was born
Inside the thigh
Of a breath: over

300 years in the grip
Of blood-drenched sweat I
Walk the flesh of the future
Like the heir's nimble
Grin at diamond dust; and my
Son playing in the nimble
Leaves of the mimosa soil-bound

Over 300 years . . . but every night
The red-lipped sun kisses the sea
The leaf mates even
With factory-filthed air
And love loves love
Bathed in a drop of the sun
Kissing the singing muscle
Of the mine labourer's son

Over 300 years of deballed grins . . .

Once-torture-twisted sighs
Of uprooted orgasms
Colour the air with riffs
Of future pulse: self-born
Maumau splits time's skull
With spearpoint flesh of mystic mask
Of built-in SHOTGUN weaved
In sounds like my daughter's

[89]

Memory of anguished joy in nigger-
Hard shadows screwing
The right moment. . . . Uptight
The raggedy-ass prophet says
Everything is alright. . . .

Origins

deep in your cheeks
your specific laughter owns
all things south of the ghosts
we once were. straight ahead
the memory beckons from the future
You and I a tribe of colours
this song that dance
godlike rhythms to birth
footsteps of memory
the very soul aspires to. songs
of origins songs of constant beginnings
what is this thing called
love

when nothing moves anywhere
the only motion is the noisy
stillness in me

should you then
                    long for
                        me
look for
   me

in forbidden songs
searching in the light
beyond petrified hypocrises

For Those who Love and Care

Who does not get what
and how not
after the descent
into points further south
of the iceboxed heart
you emerge
with pangs of rebirth
the inevitable dissent
knowing
all the thens and whens
knowing
who gets what
and how
grinning excellent madness

Remember
    When my echo upsets
    The plastic windows of your mind
    And darkness invades its artificial light
    The pieces of your regrets hard to find
                                        Remember
    I shall only be a sighing memory then
    Until you look in the fiery womb of sunrise
    Retrieving songs almost aborted
    On once battered black lips
Remember
    When you get sickandtired
    Of being sick and tired
    To remind the living
    That the dead cannot remember.

Yes, Mandela, we shall be moved
We are Men enough to have a conscience
We are Men enough to immortalize your song
We are Men enough to look Truth straight in the face

To defy the devils who traded in the human Spirit

For Black cargoes and material superprofits
We emerge to sing a Song of Fire with Roland

We emerge to prove Truth cannot be enslaved
In chains or imprisoned in an island inferno
We emerge to stand Truth on her two feet We emerge

To carry the banner of humanism across the face of the Earth

Our voice in unison with our poet's proudly says
'Change is gonna come!'

For *Afroamerica*

when your days were made
of walls cold
and whiter
than snow
when deranged vipers
Sliced through your black
genitals my body was one
huge bleeding ball.
Now
there will be no ifs
red-lipped dreams too
damned long deferred
explode
Now
redhot truths
defiant like volcanoes emerge
taller than evening shadows
from ghetto magicians
Now
from the asshole of America
gutter smells rush
the blood like
a stampede to the head
scorching centuries-long tears
up and down the land
Now
I see
Patrice and Malcolm
in your step as you
dance near the sun
your hand outstretched
to embrace that long
deferred day so close

Now
I can see
ghetto smells going
up in smoke up and down
the land exploding in
the asshole of America
I can see that day
teasing you like a whore
SCREAMING NOW.

Haartebeespoort Dam! And song and dance would pierce
the air celebrating the birth of a new year, the lyrics, with
poetic precision, caressing, describing, exploring this experience
with the robustness of released township passions. Happy New
Year . . . Happy New Year! Kwa se kusuk'amaphepha . . .
and the papers flew . . . isitimela siy'eOrlando . . . the train
going to Orlando. Yes. Mbaqanga dubbed kwela by white
critics who hear the music as nothing more than an expression
of the noisy happiness of simple-minded township natives and
a gold mine for recording companies. Fuduwa ousi . . .
Grind sister. Girl's loins right in there. Kwa suk'amaphepha.
Colossal sounds would leap out of those tiny pennywhistles
to bathe our passions in the spirit of this moment far away
from the slime of narrow, very rarely paved township streets.

Arthur Nortje

Hollows for
Travelling Music

Midnight

Tonight, precisely at that wall
my room's floor pauses in its walk,
throws up a gaze, observes the clock.
Bulb and brandy begin to talk.

Energy flows and sounds emerge,
but not from me – some alien source.
Beyond glass panels at my door
the darkness grins with utter force.

It creaked, the room's one empty chair:
devil or angel on my seat?
Outside my window, lamps bead blood
down on a tired waiting street.

The toilet gurgles by my ear,
sucks someone's paper down the drain.
Its chain keeps keeping vigilance
on odours of bowels, odours of pain.

Night after night I lie and wait
for sleep's return, but she, but she
is gripped in spastic fists of fear,
trembling at noises made by me.

Thumbing a Lift

Emaciated sand dunes and grease-black pylons
On afternoons teeming with impurities;
Brittle bitter-brown wire; the sky-blotching ravens
Must be September's electrified existences.

I live beside sap-fired willow striplings,
Yet alien to their cause, spring-exultation
Cars pass by the thin thing of my brown thumb
Rhythmically beckoning in painful indication.

Gnats swarm from scumcamps: above the asphalt
Shimmy-shaking witchdoctors gnarled like bluegums
Drunkenly perform their corrugated dazzle,
Leering through red heat with futile venom:

I scream in sad fury for movement home.
They ignore me, mama, they and their crazy
Machines, bright machines. Past this wheedling tramp
Cars swish and whizz in dust-whirling frenzy.

To be but a sliver of velocity pillioned,
Exquisitely frozen in foam-rubber pose;
Or dreamily sculptored in lavish freedom,
Trading vague pleasantries, parading poise . . .

There now, in chromium Chrysler Rambler
(Cream-leather atmosphere, cool man, relaxed)
Comes a smiling Samaritan – ah but those bulging
Ogres palm me off on an incredible next!

Trafficking with me now in truces of poison
White flags of exhaust fumes envelop my person.
So I'm afterwards only O.K. when, chosen,
A cattle truck careers me towards the horizon.

Poem

12 o'clock room with a smoke umbrella
screens me from what sad encounter?
Cold rain by my window weeping.

Wherever I stand there slants shadow,
and should I switch to darkness then
who would touch me and know I'm human?

Waters tumble and stop without reason,
wet leaves dripping. I cannot connect
this dry room with that cold rain weeping.

And each day passes with a little murmur
which I dissect each day, destroying;
those whose minds sleep in cement cells

are strange to those who rattle floorboards.
This side of this room is silent
whenever I stand and wonder why.

Windscape

Air-swept slopes of straining weed
plunge dimly to the dung-dry rocks,
shore cowers under the bilious sky.
The oil-scummed green sea heaves and slides
below my view from concrete heights
in struggle with the lurching wind.
Chopping into the curve the white surge
sprawls among boats in frothing nipples.

Sharp winds with venom flay
the brittle bones
or tug in ferocious gusts at clothes:
Rex Trueform suit from a summer shop
(what man about town, distinctive style?).
Around my limbs the wool rags bloat.

Into the lull with movement treason
I stride braced like a rod, resistance sweet.
The lash bites back, a plane of grit
sheers up obliquely. Note
how eyes squint hard into destiny's balance.

Hug
walls and walk flat and
anticipate but don't look back
or spit in the sun's pale skimming face.

The street funnels flotsam; air floats, deceptive;
black wires dirge, then, take this door.
The wild slut howls for rain
to soothe her caked and aching hollows.

Fading Light

Over the hill under fading autumn
going vehicles catching light
dart feelers back to my stand of shadows.
Around my casuals gathers evening.

Violet deepens in these shallows.
Moths tattoo the pane, obtuse, and sharp
stars glitter with malevolence.

Mere night can menace innocence
hence memory of light persists.
The blaze of grass in our last green morning:
not garish, yet enough
to grip my careless glance.

That was once, and out of nature
I craved remembrance, light-suffused.
Conversation came between us, brilliant
grass and me in smooth June:
some bland response and you travelled
on, the price of petrol? And that was once.

Shall I now meditate upon the moon?
Twice bears no thinking. Experiments, seasons,
situations alter, but their instruments, tools,
equipment, apparatus remain the same:
the leaves, reversed by the wind, acknowledge
the wisdom of the wind.
I see how from all fissures reach
your features, spreading radiance.

Apartheid

Winter parades as a mannequin.
The early scene looks virgin.
We sway past in a Volkswagen.

Nothing outwardly grieves,
so luxuriant are the trees.
Leaf-rich boughs ride past with spring's ease.

Yes, there is beauty: you make
the understandable mistake.
But the sun doesn't shine for the sun's sake.

Flame-sharp, it beats casual
sweat from my aching skull
and the May winds are mechanical.

A bird's clean flight
exhibits the virtues of light.
I skulk in a backseat, darker than white.

How should I envy the luminous
sky if the cold and anonymous
men of the world strengthen my enemies?

It matters little that
this lane, this door is separate.
In the rare air have we met.

Promise

Clock and season march, each day more mellow,
since time must nourish youth beyond the blossoms:
the new furred power glints in early patterns,
brought with true focus to your beauty now.

Words drift in multitudes from your replies,
who've chosen foreign life: I ponder snatches.
We crossed like shadows, young and watchful insects.
My time has turned to life beyond this room.

All loves have love-songs, once a girl well thought of
set spinning a lugubrious Italian.
You, mermaid with your criss-cross rain of pale
hair, never had favourites, just friends.

That sweet detachment lingers rich in influence.
O day beyond the curtain swarms with rhythms
My song to you is imminent: sky and glittering
sea and the grass of quick surprise, our world.

The luminous air presents its gifts of fragrance,
myself with its first taste in flowering spring.
The wind strays off the water with desire
among these leafing boughs to fork me open.

As I grow outward, what has held me shut,
unconscious of your vigil, you my swan?
I am as strong and fluid as a river
to give your empty spring its first fulfilment.

Athol Fugard's Invitation

Yesterday an auburn beard
at a chance encounter, again after years
your keen eyes lucent, unafraid of fear.
Discussing the country we agreed to meet
to discuss the country over wine and curry
red and strong to give us courage.

Dawn glinted early, suffusing promise
of peace to palliate our common
brooding: there would be golden company.
Sun was the sequel above a smoke-
grey cloud but then the sun-wind rose
in wisps first out of the boomering bay
or rather it swelled to occasional
gusts and broke into livid gale!

Rain beats hard against the glass,
linen flaps on a drab balcony.
Boreas batters the walls – a windy conceit
because I lack the Nordic light
illumining a surface force.

Not that I spit of deceptive lustre
(I take it in my leather complexion)
or scorn the few redeeming features.
Around me squat the sombre ruins,
the charred hulks, the bizarre
wreckage of raids and deprivations.

And to give us hope?
No rare delightful image glistens
on cobbled multi-racial pavements.
White rain beats in stinging torrents,
vehicles pass in their earnest bee-lines.

Continuation

Waking glazed into the murky dawn
and turning back into the dull body till it be day,
till it is summer or eternity:
deliberate postures hurt me.

Dim sloth aches. Numb muscles
express dumb mumbles, building
slow anger against a wall, but leave it:
brooding is deadly.
We found release in harsh liquids, bewildering.

Wry time ticks where stainless metal
nestles in ash on the stained piano.
Strange how
proud the limbs are, sprawled horizontal.

I am alone and isn't it love
to drain remains so the warmth steadily
edges along the blood, it is greedy for strength.
Love it is, lip-smudge on glass and the wine-beads
run back down the crystal. I now hear life:
alone in the room doesn't mean the whole house.

The hoarse voice searches. We compare
views of parties, find a need for food:
guts feel the acid pangs, I speak
out of passages hearing him bellow again at some staggering
    gaffe,
and continuation defeats
the bitter ascetic, despair; our words
starve that envious lusty glutton, the ego,
out of recognition: thus
we have long survived the stigma of being.

There are no more empty hollows. We
wake newly to find
sun and bird and leaf beyond in sequence:
our similar world, reassuring laughter
exploding again in an endless beginning
till it be echoed into eternity.

Song for a Passport

The nimble razor smoothed the skin,
gorging itself on lather scum.
The soap's round shoulders mollified
muscles that raged in the amorous night:
and in the new September tide
I gravitate to what is comely,
having tasted contumely
because my crust is black and hard.

In the mirror in the morning in a mood
melange such as one's swelling dream induces
I brief myself as you would were you near,
to whom my flesh was rainbow, heart was harsh.
Parting of ways exposed
love's tattered fabric
but the world rose
larger through the tears in bright enticement.

Who loves me so much not to let me go,
not to let me leave a land of problems?
O poet answer everything
so that the dull green voucher
can hold a shiny photograph
and miracles of destinations,
gold lettering endorsing many travels.

This world is grim and green, the houses
lie wrapped in mist from third-floor windows.
Glossy pages in the waiting-room feel
firm as leather and the print slides past.
Now interviews and checks are in the offing:
O ask me all but do not ask allegiance!

Transition

Aqua-clear, the bracing sky,
and morning breathes cucumber cool,
invests the leaves with gentle airs.
My final spring grows beautiful.

Most lovely, not yet being lush,
athletic grace of limb and bud.
I stand self-empty, ascetic
in this my land of wealth and blood.

For your success, black residue,
I bear desire still, night thing!
Remain in the smoky summer long
though I be gone from green-flamed spring.

Stream, Beach and Shadow : Scene

heavy, like snails, the pebbles seem to move
with a stone paleness of pain
downstream, reluctant towards the law
of gravity, the
               bank under my buttocks
is root-firm, earth's earth, and unlike

green yeast of moss in shy
patches germinating to attention
when the sky is allover blue simply
and soft, i think

With the moon gone that was
at dawn a crescent of ash
I flick sunlight off my toes
               and rise
among willow fragrances, leaves,
and the fellow-travelling shadow:
                     mute
little prisoner, the soul apologizes, how
you diminish or do you
               fear separation? hearing

the gulls scream sad abandon banking
high above the silt mouth where the mothering
sea pushes wearily lapping up
the last gift of the land.

The tide drags weed, the sea's
sore knees breed my wandering
upshore along an elbow of sand to gather
shark's-purse, washed shells, sailor's baubles, driftwood
eaten smooth
               soul white, and bluebottles

hover above the massive tunnelling waste-pipes
rust-crusted. Knives cut bait,
reefer smokers cast their ragged lines,
a tramp breaks bread, squatting to watch:
they say the glaucous mackerel
                                    bite best
there because manshit
                          has quality, is tasty

loosened roots of the bowels, though
rubber disposals are more poetic
floating gently, wombless and flat, in a rock pool

did i wonder why
                      sharks scuffle in the brown surf:
human limbs are the delicacies
                                    a careless
swimmer makes first-class offal

but the zenith sun of summer
also delivers details round the substance
of blood bone hair and fang:
where I am standing dumb my slim
shadow is quiet as a bottom circle
dark, composed, unhaloed –
                                    pared to trueness

I am blameless as a bunny in the sights of a Texas sniper,
posing on lawns among the age's infirm.
Nurses stroll arm-in-arm with grave patients,
blond in white uniforms. The air is fragrantly warm.
It is August, the era of football, the playboy summer.
In the National Shrine of the Immaculate Conception
Luci, the President's daughter, gets married, and meanwhile

Hiroshima comes of age: cool youths on Hondas
scatter the white pigeons in their path:
they are the fliers themselves, in leathers and denims.
The steel birds that shitted
mightily through the brilliant air
are junk on the scrap-heap of new generations:
the daughters radiant, silky as geishas. The late

incandescence of an unclear nuclear aura,
catching no echoes from the bomb of majority,
burned the Lucky Dragon into a coffin of white ash.
After its wandering on the clouded sea
the timbers probably rot
in some derelict dockyard of Japan.
No fish are wriggling in the glistening nets,
moonlight on the wave is sterile.

The saki did nothing for their appetite.
Pus in their eyes, their scalps brittle,
the fisherman vomited blood wearily into the green spume.
The captain lies buried on the peaceful hill
oblivious of the island's natural tremors.
I say happy birthday to the lingering victims,
dragged from my gaping chamber the morning
they suffered that prophylactic blast of atoms.

Removed, forgetful, we soon forgive
the gory orgy, whitewash the accident.
If I found a flattened city, what could I do
but scream the lust for life?
If I lay in the ashes of my dreaming days
what could I wait for but death,
untouchable in my radio-active sleep . . .

We shall survive to succumb in the megaton waves,
for now that the soul is a stone we can never be
safe enough to grant the ghosts recognition:
though we acknowledge with money and flowers
they stare us mute, the eyes appealing for passion.
Let them be nameless, those curt syllables
can never be memorable the way we are used to.

I

My teachers are dead men. I was too young
to grasp their anxieties, too nominal an exile
to mount such intensities of song;
knowing only the blond
colossus vomits its indigestible
black stepchildren like autotoxins.

Who can endure the succubus?
She who had taught them proudness of tongue
drank an aphrodisiac, then swallowed
a purgative to justify the wrong.
Her iron-fisted ogre of a son
straddled the drug-blurred townships,
breathing hygienic blasts of justice.

Rooted bacteria had their numbers
swiftly reduced in the harsh sunlight of arc-lamps,
the arid atmosphere where jackboots scrape
like crackling electric, and tape recorders
ingest forced words like white corpuscles,
until the sterile quarantine of dungeons
enveloped them with piteous oblivion.

In the towns I've acquired
arrive the broken guerrillas, gaunt and cautious,
exit visas in their rifled pockets
and no more making like Marx
for the British Museum in the nineteenth century,
damned: the dark princes, burnt and offered
to the four winds, to the salt-eyed seas. To their earth
unreturnable.

The world receives
them, Canada, England now that the laager
masters recline in a gold inertia
behind the arsenal of Sten guns. I
remember many, but especially one
almost poetic, so undeterrable.

II

He comes from knife-slashed landscapes:
I see him pounding in his youth across red sandfields
raising puffs of dust at his heels,
outclassing the geography of dongas
mapped by the ravenous thundery summers.
He glided down escarpments like the wind, until
pursued by banshee sirens
he made their wails the kernel of his eloquence,
turning for a time to irrigate
the stretches of our virgin minds.

Thus – sensitive precise
he stood with folded arms in a classroom
surveying a sea of galvanized roofs,
transfixed as a chessman, only
with deep inside his lyric brooding,
the flame-soft bitterness of love that recrudesces;
O fatal loveliness of the land
seduced the laager masters to disown us.

36,000 feet above the Atlantic
I heard an account of how they had shot
a running man in the stomach. But what isn't told
is how a warder kicked the stitches open
on a little-known island prison which used to be
a guano rock in a sea of diamond blue.

Over the phone in a London suburb he sounds
grave and patient – the years have stilled him:
the voice in a dawn of ash, moon-steady,
is wary of sunshine which has always been
more diagnostic than remedial.

The early sharpness passed beyond to noon
that melted brightly into shards of dusk.
The luminous tongue in the black world
has infinite possibilities no longer.

London Impressions

I

Out of the Whitehall shadows I pass
into a blaze of sun as sudden as fountains.
Between the bronze paws of a lion
a beatnik stretches his slack indifferent muscles.

Nelson's patina of pigeon shit
hardly oppresses that plucky sailor. Cloudbanks
lazily roll in the blue heavens beyond.
The birds home in on seas of seed.

Foil tins float on the dusty water.
The walls are full of faces and thighs.
I smoke a Gold Leaf close to the filter,
viewing dimly the circles of traffic.

The isle is full of Foreign Noises
that jangle in trafalgar square,
England expects every tourist
to do his duty now the Pound is sickly.

II

A girl plays games with mirrors
in Hyde Park while I'm half-suggestive
with the dolly scanning a volume idly.
In the flare of an instant it takes to light
a cigarette:
against her treetrunk comes to lean
the ugliest bloke that you have ever seen.
Predictably they disappear
through the distance of August green.

The nymph on the grass behind
proves her point by blinding my return look.
She picks her black bag up and drifts on further,
not helpful as to whether I should follow.
Meanwhile a huge Alsatian sniffs my loose boots,
the gentleman with the leash exchanges gossip.

Sun, you are all I have:
the grass already welcomes the brown leaves.
I do not want to cross the road again,
having learnt the value of other faces,
acquired the pace and tone of other voices.

And big red buses; I thought I would never catch
sight of the gentle monsters
when I was young and shackled for my sharpness
in the Union of South Africa.

Joy Cry

Apollo's man-breasts smooth and gold-blond
hold between in the fine-boned cleft
the kernel of radiant light. Like wind
youth's madness streams through orifices. The swift
vivacious morning shoots along the ripples:
in my loins the swelling pearl moves.

This growing jewel wants to burst
through coils and meshes the seasons have wrought.
That time can tame the green surge,
that age can quell the riotous blood,
my eyes, blind with their glory, shun.
The snow-melt waters roar down the mountain.

The joy cry of virility stirs quivers:
from your navel I bite the ivory flower.
Bud-firm, you have opened under thunder,
in your galleries my shapeless flame would dwell.
So I shall soothe your tender wound,
the one that's life-long, and unhealable.

Night Ferry

Origins – they are dim in time, colossally
locked in the terrible mountain, buried in seaslime,
or vapourized, being volatile. What purpose
has the traveller now, whose connection is cut
with the whale, the wolf or the albatross? What does your small
    mouth

tell of supernovas or of chromosomes?
There are ivory graveyards in jungled valleys,
rainbow treasures, harps that sing in the wind,
fabled wrecks where the dead sailors sleep and a cuttlefish
sleeps on a bed of old doubloons.
                           Black bows
cleave water, suffer the waves. Finding the wet
deck, funnels, covered cargo, lifeboats
roped mute above the seasurge, pit-pat beats
the heart against the rail:
my flesh of salt clings to its molecules.

Oily and endless the stream is a truth drug. Pick
up signals from vast space, gather a ghoulish cry
from an astronaut lost for ever, his electronic
panels blipping with danger signs. Below
crushed like the foil on a Cracker Barrel cheese pack
a nuclear submarine no longer muscles
into the thunderous pressure. Is it the infinite
sound I hear that's going where? and to
whom can the intelligence be given? who are you?
Not only this, but also
between us the sensory network registers
potential tones, imaginable patterns
for there are destinies as well as destinations.

Screw churns through the superstructured
centuries of shut night, washing waters:

[123]

waves dip away, swell back, break open
in froth swaths and moon cobbles.
A snatch of Bach that intervenes
fluently pours through the portholes of my ears.
Boat on the Irish waters though I hear
poignant voices, whisper of snow, spring forests.
That set up plangencies, and issue oddthoughts.
With the ephemeral melody transistored.
Your eyes also seem to feature.

O are you daylight, love, to diminish my mist?
Siren, or the breeze's child, forgetful
while reaching through my bones?
In rest rooms people crowd, sleeping fug-
postured. Anyway of whom do I think?

I find an empty bunk, bend
under the muffled light, lie
in half-sleep, knock knock goes
the who's there night – a to-fro bottle tinkles.
It is the seasway, wavespeak, dance of angles.
Listen and you listen. Those are bilge-pipes.
Some are nightsounds, far from bird cries. Or a shark's snore.
The radius of consciousness is infinite, but seesaws.

Obscene are the unborn children, insane are the destitute mothers,
I do not think, who have known them, disowned them.
The contours of cowdung, or snow in the cold hills
criss-crossing earthwards, or zigzag catgut
stitches on chest incisions – these are the merely
straightline rhythms, level planes, the simplicity ratio.
Then there's you
who must somewhere exist to be regarded
as needy, needed, night-bound: a cherished enigma.

Waiting

The isolation of exile is a gutted
warehouse at the back of pleasure streets:
the waterfront of limbo stretches panoramically –
night the beautifier lets the lights
dance across the wharf.
I peer through the skull's black windows
wondering what can credibly save me.
The poem trails across the ruined wall
a solitary snail, or phosphorescently
swims into vision like a fish
through a hole in the mind's foundation, acute
as a glittering nerve.

Origins trouble the voyager much, those roots
that have sipped the waters of another continent.
Africa is gigantic, one cannot begin
to know even the strange behaviour furthest
south in my xenophobic department.
Come back, come back mayibuye
cried the breakers of stone and cried the crowds
cried Mr. Kumalo before the withering fire
mayibuye Afrika

Now there is the loneliness of lost
beauties at Cabo de Esperancia, Table Mountain:
all the dead poets who sang of spring's
miraculous recrudescence in the sandscapes of Karoo
sang of thoughts that pierced like arrows, spoke
through the strangled throat of multi-humanity
bruised like a python in the maggot-fattening sun.

You with your face of pain, your touch of gaiety,
with eyes that could distil me any instant

have passed into some diary, some dead journal
now that the computer, the mechanical notion
obliterates sincerities.
The amplitude of sentiment has brought me no nearer
to anything affectionate,
new magnitude of thought has but betrayed
the lustre of your eyes.

You yourself have vacated the violent arena
for a northern life of semi-snow
under the Distant Early Warning System:
I suffer the radiation burns of silence.
It is not cosmic immensity or catastrophe
that terrifies me:
it is solitude that mutilates,
the night bulb that reveals ash on my sleeve.

Immigrant

Don't travel beyond
Acton at noon in the intimate summer light
of England

to Tuskaloosa, Medicine Hat, preparing
for flight

dismissing the blond aura of the past
at Durban or Johannesburg
no more chewing roots or brewing riots

Bitter costs exorbitantly at London
airport in the neon heat
waiting for the gates to open

Big boy breaking out of the masturbatory
era goes
like eros over atlantis (sunk
in the time-repeating seas, admire our
tenacity)
jetting into the bulldozer civilization
of Fraser and Mackenzie
which is the furthest west that man has gone

A maple leaf is in my pocket.
X-rayed, doctored at Immigration
weighed in at the Embassy
measured as to passport, smallpox, visa
at last the efficient official informs me
I am an acceptable soldier of fortune, don't

tell the Commissioner
I have Oxford poetry in the satchel

propped between my army surplus boots
for as I consider Western Arrow's
pumpkin pancake buttered peas and chicken canadian style
in my mind's customs office
questions fester that turn the menu
into a visceral whirlpool. You can see
that sick bags are supplied.

Out portholes beyond the invisible propellers
snow mantles the ground peaks over Greenland.
What ice island of the heart has weaned
you away from the known white kingdom
first encountered at Giant's Castle?
You walked through the proteas nooked in the sun rocks
I approached you under the silver trees.
I was cauterized in the granite glare
on the slopes of Table Mountain, I was baffled
by the gold dumps of the vast Witwatersrand
when you dredged me from the sea like a recent fossil.

Where are the mineworkers, the compound Africans,
your Zulu ancestors, where are
the root-eating, bead-charmed Bushmen, the Hottentot sufferers?
Where are the governors and sailors of the
Dutch East India Company, where are
Eva and the women who laboured in the castle?
You are required as an explanation.

Glaciers sprawl in their jagged valleys,
cool in the heights, there are mountains and mountains.
My prairie beloved, you whose eyes are
less forgetful, whose fingers are less oblivious
must write out chits for the physiotherapy customers
must fill out forms for federal tax.

Consolatory, the air whiskies my veins.
The metal engines beetle on to further destinations.
Pilot's voice reports over Saskatchewan
the safety of this route, the use of exits,
facility of gas masks, Western Arrow's
miraculous record. The flat sea washes
in Vancouver bay. As we taxi in
I find I can read the road signs.

Maybe she is like you, maybe most women
deeply resemble you, all of them are
all things to all poets: the cigarette girl
in velvet with mink nipples, fishnet thighs,
whose womb is full of tobacco.
Have a B.C. apple in the A.D. city of the saviour,
and sing the centennial song.

Biographical Notes

DOLLAR BRAND was born and educated in Cape Town. He matriculated from Trafalgar High School in Cape Town's District Six. Brand is a widely known jazz pianist and composer and has worked in both Cape Town and Johannesburg. In 1960 he went to Europe with a small group of musicians and they played mainly in Switzerland and Scandinavia. After about six years Brand moved to the U.S.A., returning to South Africa in 1968.

Now in his mid-thirties, Brand is married to the singer Bea Benjamin. He has been writing verse for the last six or seven years. This group first appeared in *The Journal of the New African Literature and Arts*.

DENNIS BRUTUS was born in Salisbury, Rhodesia, of South African parents in 1924. He graduated from Fort Hare in 1947 with a distinction in English. He lived and taught in Port Elizabeth until he was banned from attending any public assemblies in 1961. After eighteen months hard labour and a year under house arrest for his opposition to apartheid, Brutus emigrated from South Africa in 1966. He has travelled widely as an author, political figure and sports enthusiast. He now lives in London with his family. He is Director of the World Campaign for the Release of South African Political Prisoners, and is President of the South African Non-Racial Olympic Committee which has successfully campaigned for South Africa's exclusion from the Olympic Games.

Dennis Brutus has published two volumes of poetry, *Sirens, Knuckles, Boots* (Mbari, 1964) and *Letters to Martha* (Heinemann, 1968). His poems have appeared in numerous magazines, newspapers and anthologies in Africa, Europe and the U.S.A. and have been translated into various languages. Critical articles on his work are to be found, among others, in *Black Orpheus, Transition, The Journal of the New African Literature and Arts* and *River Forest Review*. His appearances in English anthologies include *Modern Poetry from Africa* (Penguin, 1968), *South*

African Writing Today (Penguin, 1967) and *African–English Literature* (Peter Owen).

Poems have been published in: *Black Orpheus, Transition, Encounter, Breakthru, Christian Action, The New African, Africa Today, African Arts/Arts D'Afrique, African Freedom News, Tribune, Purple Renoster, The Journal of the New African Literature and Arts, Presence Africaine, Mayibuye, Sechaba* and produced for broadcasting by: Radio Deutsche Welle and The Transcription Centre.

I. CHOONARA was born in Roodepoort, Transvaal, and has been living in the United Kingdom since 1954.

A graduate of London University he has worked as a research chemist with the Gas Council followed by a six-year spell as a mathematics teacher. He recently gained the Master's degree and is currently engaged in further post-graduate work and combining it with writing and painting. A number of short stories and poems have appeared in various publications on both sides of the Atlantic including the *Christian, Sennet, Transatlantic Review, African Arts/Arts D'Afrique* and *The New African*, and has had plays produced for broadcasting.

C. J. DRIVER comes from the Transvaal. He went to the University of Cape Town and was president of the National Union of South African Students in 1963 and 1964.

After being detained under the old ninety-day detention law he left South Africa for England. He went to Trinity College, Oxford, to read for a B.Phil. and is now housemaster of the International Sixth Form Centre at Sevenoaks School.

His poems have appeared in the collections *London Magazine Poems, New South African Writing* (P.E.N.), *South African Writing Today* (Penguin) and in Uys Krige and Jack Cope's *Book of South African Verse* (Penguin). His poems have also been published in: *The Lion and the Impala, The New African, New Coin, Contrast, The London Magazine, Tracks, Caliban* and *Solstice*.

His first novel, *Elegy for a Revolutionary*, was published by Faber and Faber in 1969. His second *Send War in Our Time, O Lord*, was published in 1970.

TIMOTHY HOLMES was born in 1936 in Johannesburg. He went to school in Pietermaritzburg and then to Trinity College, Oxford. He was assistant editor of *Contact* until he went to teach in Zambia. He is now living in Lusaka.

His work has appeared in *The New African and Contrast*.

KEORAPETSE KGOSITSILE was born in Johannesburg thirty-one years ago, and has lived in exile for about ten years. He is at present on the staff of *Black Dialogue Magazine* in New York. He first went to the United States in 1962 and has studied at Lincoln University, the University of Hampshire, Columbia University in the creative writers' workshop, and at the New School of Social Research in New York.

Kgositsile's work, criticism and poetry, has been published in *Présence Africaine*, *The Journal of the New African Literature and the Arts*, *Transition* and *The New African*.

Two volumes of his poetry have been published in the U.S.A.: *Spirits Unchained* and *For Melba*.

ARTHUR NORTJE was born in Port Elizabeth. He went to the segregated University College of the Western Cape and then, after a short period of teaching English in South Africa, read English at Jesus College, Oxford. In 1967 he went to teach in Canada.

He won a prize in the 1962 Mbari Literary Competition sponsored by the Congress for Cultural Freedom based in Paris. He has been included in the revised and enlarged edition of *Modern Poetry from Africa* (Poetry). His poetry has appeared in *Black Orpheus*, *African Arts Arts D'Afrique*, the *Anglo-Welsh Review*, and various little magazines.